I0142577

THE
PROCESS
EQUALS
THE
PRODUCT

FORWARD PROGRESS ONE STEP AT A TIME

WORKBOOK

T. DWAYNE SMITH, SR., M.A., CLC

The Process Equals the Product:
Workbook
Second Print Edition
ISBN 13: 978-0-9908109-1-9
Copyright © 2016 T. Dwayne Smith, Sr., M.A., CLC

Unless otherwise indicated, all Scripture quotations are taken from the King James Version of the Bible. Scriptures noted AMP are taken from the Amplified® Bible, Copyright © 1954, 1958, 1962, 1964, 1965, 1987 by The Lockman Foundation
Used by permission. Scriptures noted NIV are taken from the HOLY BIBLE: NEW INTERNATIONAL VERSION®. Copyright © 1973, 1978, 1984 by International Bible Society. Used by permission of Zondervan Publishing House. All rights reserved. Scriptures noted GNT are taken from the Good News Translation® (Today's English Version, Second Edition) Copyright © 1992 American Bible Society. All rights reserved. Use by permission.

All photographs are open source distributed under a CC-BY 2.0 license.

Printed in the United States of America.
All rights reserved under International Copyright Law. Contents and / or cover may not be reproduced in whole or in part in any form without the express written consent of the author.

This workbook is the companion book to "The Process Equals the Product" available online or by request wherever books are sold.

Team Unstoppable, Inc.
444 E. Roosevelt, Rd., Suite #254 Lombard, IL 60148 | 708.218.1104

contents

chapter one

MY PROCESS

Self-Reflection / Life Application

"You are special, unique and you will make a positive contribution to this world!"
- Mr. Coleman
Teacher: J. Sterling Morton Middle School, Chicago, IL

1. Take a moment and reflect on a personal challenge you may have had or may be currently experiencing. This challenge may be personal, academic, or relational. Describe this challenge in detail.

_____

_____

_____

_____

_____

_____

_____

_____

2. What has been your attitude/approach to dealing with personal challenges? Have you allowed the challenge to become a barrier to stop your forward progress and personal success?

_____

_____

_____

_____

_____

_____

3. How has your personal challenges influenced your decision and choices in life (positive/ negative)? Please share both positive and negative decisions and choices.

_____
_____
_____
_____
_____
_____
_____

4. The writer talks about the correlation between environmental factors and thinking/ behavior. The writer also utilizes the illustration of the Piranha and the Goldfish to demonstrate the impact of environmental factors and behavior. Please share some environmental factors you believe are influencing your thinking and behavior.

_____
_____
_____
_____
_____
_____
_____

5. Reflecting on these environmental factors, which factors are stifling, containing, and limiting your potential? What can you do to change these factors?

_____
_____
_____
_____
_____
_____
_____
_____
_____
_____

6. When you talk about your personal challenges, are you positive or negative?

_____

_____

_____

_____

_____

_____

_____

_____

_____

_____

7. Think about a personal challenge/struggles, then circle the word that best describes your outlook regarding your situation 9 out of 10 times?

OPTIMISTIC   PESSIMISTIC

8. If you circled pessimistic, what can you do personally or what help can you seek to change your perspective and approach to your situation from pessimistic to optimistic?

_____

_____

_____

_____

_____

_____

_____

_____

_____

_____

_____

_____

_____

9. Think about a personal accomplishment in your life and share why you feel proud of this accomplishment.

_____
_____
_____
_____
_____
_____
_____

10. The writer shared his personal process. Now, reflect on your process and share how you can grow and become a better person through your experience.

_____
_____
_____
_____
_____
_____
_____
_____
_____
_____
_____
_____
_____

11. Before making any decision, no matter how big or small the writer recommends that you follow four steps. Write the four steps below and share why you think these steps are important in making decisions in your life.

1. _____
2. _____
3. _____
4. _____

12. What are some of your personal fears? How do you deal with fear? Please explain.

_____

_____

_____

_____

_____

_____

_____

_____

_____

_____

_____

_____

_____

_____

_____

reflective notes

chapter two

THE ENEMY OF EXCELLENCE IS AVERAGE

Self-Reflection / Life Application

"Average is half as good as the best, twice as good as the worst!"
- John Avanzani
Evangelist

1. In your own words define "average."

_____
_____
_____
_____
_____
_____
_____

2. In your own words define "excellence."

_____
_____
_____
_____
_____
_____
_____
_____

3. Do you consider yourself *average* or *excellent*? Explain in detail why you see yourself this way.

_____
_____
_____
_____
_____
_____
_____

4. If you view yourself as average, what can you do to elevate your thinking out of a place of average into a place of excellence?

_____
_____
_____
_____
_____
_____
_____
_____
_____
_____
_____
_____
_____
_____
_____

5. List three to five gifts or talents that you believe God has placed within you.

_____
_____
_____
_____
_____
_____
_____

6. Which of the three to five gifts are you currently utilizing?

_____
_____
_____
_____
_____
_____
_____

7. How do you see your gift(s) elevating you into personal and professional success?

_____
_____
_____
_____
_____
_____
_____
_____
_____
_____
_____

8. In what ways do you see your gift(s) being a benefit to others and the world?

_____
_____
_____
_____
_____
_____
_____
_____
_____
_____
_____
_____
_____
_____

9. Think about the quote on page 66, "birds of the same feather flock together." What does that mean to you and how can you apply this principle to your friendships/associations?

_____
_____
_____
_____
_____
_____
_____

10. An "accountability partner" is a person you trust and will hold you accountable to achieving your dreams, goals and aspirations in life. Do you have anybody in your circle of friends that you would consider as an accountability partner? If so, name the individual(s) and share why you trust them.

_____
_____
_____
_____
_____
_____
_____

11. Fill in the blanks with positive words that describe you.

I am _____
I am _____
I am _____
I am _____
I am _____
I am _____
I am _____
I am _____

12. List five people who inspire you.

1. _____
2. _____
3. _____
4. _____
5. _____

13. List some of their positive character traits.

_____
_____
_____
_____
_____
_____
_____
_____
_____
_____

14. What aspects of their lives would you like to model in your personal/professional life?

_____
_____
_____
_____
_____
_____
_____
_____
_____
_____
_____
_____
_____
_____
_____

reflective notes

chapter three

THE DISTORTED IMAGE

Self-Reflection / Life Application

"Opportunity is missed by most people because it is dressed in overalls and looks like work!"

- Thomas A. Edison
Scientist and Inventor

1. List five adjectives that describe you.

1. _____
2. _____
3. _____
4. _____
5. _____

2. If I were to interview four of your closest friends, what would they say about you?

_____
_____
_____
_____
_____
_____
_____
_____
_____
_____

Reflection Questions/ Recognizing Your Value

3. List five people that are very influential in your life.

1. _____
2. _____
3. _____
4. _____
5. _____

4. In the space below, list the names of the 5 people from your inner circle and place a (+) next to the person's name if you feel that this relationship has a positive influence on your life or a (-) if you feel that this relationship has a negative influence in your life.

_____
_____
_____
_____
_____
_____
_____
_____
_____
_____
_____

5. Review your list of people you consider to be positive influences and write what characteristics and/or qualities about them make them a positive influence.

_____
_____
_____
_____
_____
_____
_____
_____
_____

6. If you could take all five of the people you listed above and place them into one person, how would you describe that one person? What personal qualities do you share with this "one" person?

_____
_____
_____
_____
_____
_____
_____
_____

7. What lasting impression would you want people to have about you?

_____
_____
_____
_____
_____
_____
_____
_____
_____

8. List the qualities you look for in people falling in each category:

Friends: _____
_____
_____

Family: _____
_____
_____

Co-Workers: _____
_____

9. Do you attract "chickens" or "eagles"?

_____
_____
_____
_____
_____
_____
_____

10. How has your (self-image) positively or negatively impacted your decision making and the direction you have chosen for your life?

_____
_____
_____
_____
_____
_____
_____
_____

11. Identify and list any trauma/stress in your life that may have negatively impacted your self-esteem. As a result of the trauma/stress in your life, do you see yourself like the eagle who was stuck in the chicken yard or the eagle who was free to express his true value and potential?

_____
_____
_____
_____
_____
_____
_____
_____
_____
_____
_____

12. List negative thought patterns about yourself.

_____
_____
_____
_____
_____
_____
_____
_____

13. What are you doing about the negative thoughts?

_____
_____
_____
_____
_____
_____
_____

14. List three people that you can open up and talk to honestly about yourself.

1. _____
2. _____
3. _____

15. Make your own "T" chart similar to the one used to identify the differences between the eagle and chicken in the book. List all negative thought patterns and negative words that have been used to describe you. On the other side, list the opposite / positive words to replace the negative words.

negative qualities / thoughts / images of myself	the opposite of that image would be...

Look at the simple four-step process for changing your self-image from negative to positive and complete the activities.

1. **Step One:** *Realize you need to change.* In one sentence admit that there are changes you need to make about your self-image to propel you into a successful life.

   _____

   _____

   _____

   _____

   _____

   _____

2. **Step Two:** *Make a firm decision to change.* Finish this sentence, "Today I will change.....

   _____

   _____

   _____

   _____

   _____

   _____

3. **Step Three:** *Evaluate your associations/environments and remove all chickens.* List any and all negative associations and environments that are potential barriers to forward progress.

   _____

   _____

   _____

   _____

   _____

   _____

4. **Step**

   Four: *Stay committed to your decision to change no matter how uncomfortable.* Here is where the accountability partner can make a BIG difference. Ask your accountability partner to help you remain on task and committed to the change process. Once you change how you see yourself, you can change your associations and the direction of your life. It is your responsibility to "become" what God has ordained you to be, SUCCESS-FUL! Journal your process in the reflection journal note section of the workbook.

Distorted Image Self-Assessment

Below are 20 statements. Read each statement and think about how strongly that statement reflects how you see yourself. Remember that honesty is the best policy, so please be honest in your responses so you can benefit from the assessment results.

Instructions:

Place a number (1- 5) next to the statement that best describes your current self-image. Then, add the total points to get your assessment score. See scoring results on the following page.

1 = No; I do not see myself this way at all!
2 = Not really sure if I see myself this way.
3 = Sometimes I see myself this way.
4 = Yes, this is me most of the time.
5 = Yes, this is exactly how I see myself!

___ I have high standards for myself.
___ I see myself as successful and confident.
___ I am achieving my dreams in life.
___ When I look in the mirror I see someone I admire.
___ When I envision my future, I see myself being successful and happy.
___ The environment around me (or My environment) is positive, supportive and healthy.
___ I make it a priority to be a positive influence to those around me.
___ I have a solid spiritual relationship with God.
___ I make it my priority to eat healthy.
___ Being physically fit and healthy is important to me.
___ I see myself like an eagle, soaring to new heights and freely achieving my goals.
___ I embrace my gifts and talents and I use them in a positive way.
___ I fully understand my purpose.
___ I don't let my peers or the opinions of others negatively impact my life and bring me down.
___ When I communicate with other people, my words are encouraging, uplifting, and positive.
___ I have overcome trauma and major stressors of my life and do not allow them to pull me into a helpless state of thinking.
___ When placed in stressful situations, I remain calm because I know I have stamina, endurance, and confidence to work through the situation.
___ I feel that I know who I am and I am comfortable and confident in my abilities.

___ I surround myself with people who are positive, successful and encouraging.

___ I see myself as teachable, humble, and always willing to learn new things to better myself.

_____ Total Points (Assessment Score, see below for explanation)

100 – 90: NO Distortion Here!!

Good Job! Stay encouraged and continue to use this workbook as a tool and set new benchmarks for yourself as you continue to climb to the next level of success.

89 - 75: Slightly Distorted

Overall, you are a positive person and you have a healthy outlook of yourself. Continue to use this workbook to build your self-image and to become the "eagle" your were meant to be.

74 - 55: Moderately Distorted

You seem to be on the fence about yourself, sometimes you are positive and sometimes you are handling the stress of life from a negative outlook. Don't allow any distorted image of yourself to stop you from achieving your true potential! You are created with so much greatness in you. As you answer the questions in this workbook, take an honest look at yourself and get off the fence! Make more statements of positive affirmation about yourself and start living your life with purpose. Allow no more room for negative images of yourself. You are valuable; you can do this!

54 - 20: Severely Distorted!

My friend you have work to do. The good news is you have started the process of change. Now, stay committed! Change will not come over time but you have to remain patience. Continue to read "The Process Equals The Process" and study the principals highlighted in the book. See yourself as the finished "Product" now and stay committed to the "Process!

reflective notes

chapter four

ATTITUDE DETERMINES ALTITUDE

Self-Reflection / Life Application

"Ability is what you're capable of doing.
Motivation determines what you do.
Attitude determines how well you do it."
- Raymond Chandler

1. Review the quotes at the beginning of chapter 4 in the book and identify the one quote that resonates with you. Write the quote down and share why this quote is impactful to you.

_____

_____

_____

_____

_____

_____

_____

2. Now, write your own quote or personal affirmation that best reflects your attitude and perspective of life.

_____

_____

_____

_____

_____

3. When you have the right attitude, you position yourself for three things to happen in your life. List these three things.

1. _____
2. _____
3. _____

4. How do you think these three things can make your life more fulfilling?

_____
_____
_____
_____
_____
_____
_____
_____

5. Who is your role model? What type of attitude do they have about life? What type(s) of adversity did they have to overcome to achieve success?

_____
_____
_____
_____
_____
_____
_____
_____

6. Has anyone ever told you that you should improve your attitude? Did you respond in a negative or positive way? Take a moment and journal your thoughts about the conversation or incident.

_____
_____
_____
_____
_____
_____
_____

7. Do you think you have a mindset that is open towards correction?

YES   NO

8. People who refuse to take responsibility for their attitudes lack maturity. Do you agree with this statement? Why or why not?

9. Have you ever had a supervisor with a REALLY bad attitude? How did their attitude impact your work performance? Describe this experience in detail.

10. If you had a friend who had a really bad attitude, what advice would you offer this person to improve his or her attitude?

When you start to feel pressure and stress, do you notice that your attitude changes? Do you become more irritable? If so, please see the tips below on how to overcome a negative attitude.

Tips for overcoming a negative attitude:

- Think positive and stay positive.
- Find a Bible scripture, quote, or song that helps to change your attitude, then say, recite, or sing it to yourself.
- Think about something that makes you happy.
- Surround yourself with positive people and hang out with them (locate the "eagles," stay away from the "chickens").
- Focus on the message and not the tune.
- See yourself as victorious!
- Look for an opportunity to serve others.
- Remind yourself that you are a work in progress.
- Find humor in every situation.
- Laugh at yourself.
- Be THANKFUL.
- Stay away from "chicken" talk!
- And always remember the three R's
  1. Relax
  2. Reflect
  3. Release

Use "I" Statements:

"I can do anything!"

"I can be anything!"

"I am not defined by situations, circumstances, or people!"

"I can't fail!"

"I will have a good attitude!"

"I will be successful!"

"I will not allow fear to contain me!"

"I am who God says I am!"

"I am Unstoppable!"

Applying the Positive Attitude Principal (PAP) read the scenarios below and answer the following questions.

A. Patricia was new in town and was invited to a social event by her close and dear friend Maria. When Maria and Patricia arrived to the event, Maria wandered off to talk and socialize with other friends and never returned to check on Patricia. After a couple of hours of being alone and becoming overwhelmed with frustration and disappointment, Patricia decided to leave the event and go home. How would you deal with this situation in a positive way?

_____
_____
_____
_____
_____
_____
_____
_____
_____
_____

B. Terrell is the assigned leader of a study group in his class. The group agreed to meet weekly in preparation for their paper and presentation for class. After the first meeting, the group decided to divide up and share responsibilities among all the team members. Terrell begin to notice that nobody in the group was fulfilling their responsibilities, with the exception of himself and one other teammate. The group has less than two weeks to complete the project before the MANDATORY deadline. Fifty percent of the grade is to be based on synergy (teamwork) and the remaining 50% is to be based on the research paper. What attitude should Terrell take? How would you advise Terrell to successfully motivate his group to complete the project and meet their deadline?

_____
_____
_____
_____
_____
_____
_____
_____
_____

reflective notes

chapter five

FINISH THE WORK

Self-Reflection / Life Application

> *"Defeat doesn't finish a man, quit does. A man is not finished when he's defeated. He's finished when he quits."*
> - Richard M. Nixon

The process is the _____, work is the _____.

1. The writer says, "failure is the other side of success." What does this mean to you?

_____

_____

_____

_____

_____

_____

_____

_____

_____

2. Is it challenging for you to make and keep personal/professional commitments? Do you find it difficult to meet deadlines and complete projects? Please explain why you may think it's a challenge for you in this area.

_____

_____

_____

_____

_____

_____

_____

_____

_____

_____

_____

3. Think about the Michael Jordan quote, "I've failed over, and over, and over again in my life and that is why I succeed." Why is this significant and how can you apply this principle to your life?

_____

_____

_____

_____

_____

_____

_____

_____

4. List three tasks/challenges that you believed you failed at in your life.

1. _____
2. _____
3. _____

5. Reflecting on your failures, what have you learned about yourself and how can you turn these failures into successes?

_____

_____

_____

_____

_____

_____

_____

6. The process brings with it three moments. As described in the text, what are these three moments:

_____

_____

_____

_____

_____

_____

_____

_____

7. Why are these moments important for the completion of the product?

_____

_____

_____

_____

_____

_____

_____

_____

_____

_____

8. The writer talks about the "wilderness experience." Explain the writer's perspective of the "wilderness experience" as it pertains to a season in your life.

_____

_____

_____

_____

_____

_____

_____

_____

_____

_____

9. Reflect on your "wilderness experience," and share how this experience impacted your life.

_____

_____

_____

_____

_____

_____

_____

10. Why is legacy so important? What type of legacy will you leave for your children?

_____

_____

_____

_____

_____

_____

_____

_____

11. What is the irony of the statement, "Become a graveyard digger?"

_____

_____

_____

_____

_____

12. Write the scripture for II Corinthians 8:11 and share in your own words what you think this scripture means.

_____

_____

_____

_____

_____

_____

13. How does this scripture relate to your life and what can you draw from this scripture to encourage you in your own personal life / situation?

_____

_____

_____

_____

_____

_____

_____

_____

14. Look at the puzzle analogy and fill in the blanks with any unfinished projects and assignments in your life that will complete your picture.

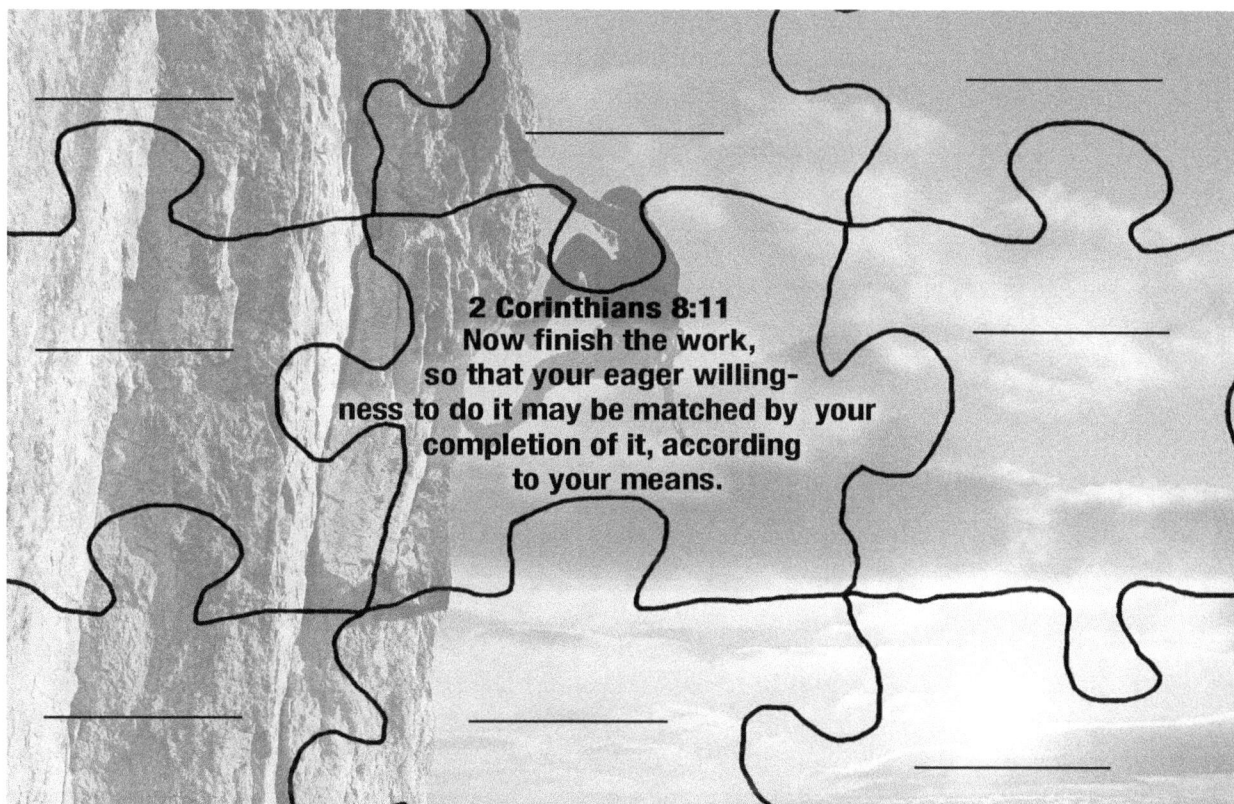

2 Corinthians 8:11
Now finish the work,
so that your eager willing-
ness to do it may be matched by your
completion of it, according
to your means.

reflective notes

chapter six

THE WORK – MY PRODUCT

Self-Reflection / Life Application

"The end of something is better than its beginning."
- Ecclesiastes 7:8 (NLT)

What spectacular things are you holding back from the world?

What do you dream about?

What do you talk about?

Who do you want to be in life?

What burning desire(s) do you have?

Your God-given potential is limitless!

You are AWESOME!

Become The Product You Were Created To Be!

Every person and every experience that you have encountered has directly impacted, shaped and influenced the person you are today. This is your process! You are the sum total of your life experiences and relationships. That is your product! If you are not happy with your product, change your process!

The Process Equals the Product.

Success is on the inside of you and it's your responsibility to work success from the inside out! Release your potential for greatness - The Product!

"The Product" where you put your plans into action!

The Process Equals The Product - Goal Setting

I have three very important questions for you to answer:

1. Do you know what you want in life?
2. Do you understand the process that is required to obtain your personal, professional, and financial dreams?
3. Have you written your vision and made it plain?

If not, why not?

_____

_____

_____

_____

_____

_____

_____

_____

_____

"Nothing can stop the man with the right mental attitude from achieving his goal; nothing on earth can help the man with the wrong mental attitude."
- *Thomas Jefferson*

My Product!

(Pray Mark 11:22-24 - Believe God)

My Ultimate Goal:

_____

_____

_____

_____

_____

_____

_____

Write 3 goals: (1) Short-Term, (1) Mid-Term, and (1) Long-Term that you want to accomplish in your life.

1. _____
2. _____
3. _____

Action Plan:

Short-term Plan (1 month – 3 months)

1. _____
2. _____
3. _____

Mid-term Plan (3 months – 9 months)

1. _____
2. _____
3. _____

Long-term Plan (9 months – 3 years)

1. _____
2. _____
3. _____

Accountability Partner Pledge

Accountability Partner X_____Date_____/_____/_____

Accountability Partner: X_____Date_____/_____/_____

At the end of every year for the next 3 years, Review, Assess, and Adjust your goals. Use the product goal chart below as a guide to set SMART GOALS and to stay accountable. Remove this page, provide a copy to your Accountability Partner and place it in a frequently visible location as a constant reminder.

	Description	Action	Follow Up	Date of completion
P	**Promise to complete the goal!** Make a promise to yourself and others to complete this goal and stick to it!	The People I will allow to hold me accountable to this goal are:	I plan to follow up with this person every:	
R	**Reasonable goals are reachable goals!** Make small achievable goals that lead up to the BIG goal!	Make a list of the smaller goals and deadlines that need to be set to achieve the main goal.	Pick a day of the week to follow up on these goals, mark them complete as you finish them, and set new ones.	
O	**Open yourself up to making adjustments.** Your goal may change slightly from time to time as you work toward the final product.	Make notation of how you can predict how your goal outcomes may change.	Follow up by the date you set to see how the goal is progressing and how any new insights have impacted the goal.	
D	**Determination!!!** The road may get bumpy...but stay determined.	List ways you will keep yourself encouraged to accomplish the goal. (Reward yourself)	Establish reward dates for meeting my goals:	
U	**Understand that there is work required!**	List the requirements or commitments to obtain this goal.	Follow-up work that needs to be done on a weekly basis.	
C	**Commitment**	List ways you will keep yourself accountable to your goals.	Check your progress every two weeks. Always ask yourself, "Am I on track?"	
T	**Time Management is the key!**	Set timelines to manage your goals.	Beware of time wasters / distractions that may hinder your forward progress and completion of goals.	

The P.R.O.D.U.C.T. Goal Chart is a tool that is used to identify what you want, establish a plan to attain what you want, and to set timelines to accomplish what you want.

Read each column of the P.R.O.D.U.C.T. Goal Chart and follow suggested expectations for each individual goal you set for yourself.

Other Suggested Goal Topics:

1. **Spiritual Goals:** What is your relationship with God and how would you like to improve that relationship?

_____
_____
_____
_____
_____
_____

2. **Career Goals:** What type of career do you want? How much money would you like to make? What age would you like to retire?

_____
_____
_____
_____
_____
_____

3. **Financial Goals:** How much money would you like to have in your savings account? What does your financial portfolio look like?

_____
_____
_____
_____
_____

4. **Educational Goals:** Where will you attend college? What subject do you want to study? What is the highest level of education you would like to obtain?

_____
_____
_____
_____
_____
_____
_____
_____

5. **Relationship Goals:** What type of relationship would you like to have with your family, significant other, children, friends?

_____
_____
_____
_____
_____
_____
_____
_____
_____

List 3 people who will stand with you in prayer and hold you accountable to accomplish your goals:

1. _____
2. _____
3. _____

Write your personal vision affirmation.

_____
_____
_____
_____
_____

Where do you see yourself (The Product) in the next 10-15 years?

Use the **I.P.D.E.** Method.

Identify all the situations and circumstances in your life.

Predict all the possible outcomes of the situations and circumstances based on your choices.

Decide on the outcome you desire that is also consistent with the vision God has given you for your life.

Execute your decision and commit to "the Process" until you become "the Product."

_____
_____
_____
_____
_____
_____
_____
_____
_____
_____
_____
_____
_____
_____
_____
_____

What is New about Me?

Based on what you have learned about yourself as a result of reading this book, write five new things you have learned.

1. _____
2. _____
3. _____
4. _____
5. _____

Finish the Work Personal Accountability Exercise:

Write down five goals or dreams that you attempted to accomplish, but for whatever reason did not. Set your new deadlines.

1. _____(Date)_____/_____/_____

2. _____(Date)_____/_____/_____

3. _____(Date)_____/_____/_____

4. _____(Date)_____/_____/_____

5. _____(Date)_____/_____/_____

reflective notes

SCHOOL / WORK ORGANIZER   DATE

MAJOR PROJECT

TODAY'S GOALS   **MIT***

○_____: ☆

○_____: ☆

○_____: ☆

○_____: ☆

○_____: ☆

○_____: ☆

○_____: ☆

○_____: ☆

○_____: ☆

○_____: ☆

*An MIT is a "Most Important Thing" Wirte only 10 things—Why try to do more? You'll be discouraged

TOMMOROW'S OBJECTIVE   **PRE-SCHEDULED MEETINGS**

NOTES, THOUGHTS, REFLECTIONS:

PROCESS = PRODUCT

SCHOOL / WORK ORGANIZER   DATE

MAJOR PROJECT

TODAY'S GOALS   **MIT***

○_____: ☆

○_____: ☆

○_____: ☆

○_____: ☆

○_____: ☆

○_____: ☆

○_____: ☆

○_____: ☆

○_____: ☆

○_____: ☆

*An MIT is a "Most Important Thing" Wirte only 10 things—Why try to do more? You'll be discouraged

TOMMOROW'S OBJECTIVE   **PRE-SCHEDULED MEETINGS**

NOTES, THOUGHTS, REFLECTIONS:

PROCESS = PRODUCT

SCHOOL / WORK ORGANIZER   DATE

MAJOR PROJECT

TODAY'S GOALS   **MIT***

○_____: ☆

○_____: ☆

○_____: ☆

○_____: ☆

○_____: ☆

○_____: ☆

○_____: ☆

○_____: ☆

○_____: ☆

○_____: ☆

***An MIT is a "Most Important Thing" Wirte only 10 things—Why try to do more? You'll be discouraged**

TOMMOROW'S OBJECTIVE   **PRE-SCHEDULED MEETINGS**

NOTES, THOUGHTS, REFLECTIONS:

PROCESS = PRODUCT

ASSIGNMENT / ACTIVITY ORGANIZER DATE

TODAY'S GOAL

TODAY'S ACTIVITIES / ASSIGNMENTS / PROJECTS   MIT*

○ _____ : ☆

○ _____ : ☆

○ _____ : ☆

○ _____ : ☆

○ _____ : ☆

○ _____ : ☆

○ _____ : ☆

○ _____ : ☆

○ _____ : ☆

○ _____ : ☆

*An MIT is a "Most Important Thing" Wirte only 10 things—Why try to do more? You'll be discouraged

ME-TIME

PRE-SCHEDULED MEETINGS

REFLECTIONS, MEDITATIONS, THOUGHTS

PROCESS = PRODUCT

ASSIGNMENT / ACTIVITY ORGANIZER DATE

TODAY'S GOAL

TODAY'S ACTIVITIES / ASSIGNMENTS / PROJECTS   **MIT***

O_____: ☆

O_____: ☆

O_____: ☆

O_____: ☆

O_____: ☆

O_____: ☆

O_____: ☆

O_____: ☆

O_____: ☆

O_____: ☆

*An MIT is a "Most Important Thing" Wirte only 10 things—Why try to do more? You'll be discouraged

ME-TIME   **PRE-SCHEDULED MEETINGS**

REFLECTIONS, MEDITATIONS, THOUGHTS

PROCESS = PRODUCT

ASSIGNMENT / ACTIVITY ORGANIZER DATE

TODAY'S GOAL

TODAY'S ACTIVITIES / ASSIGNMENTS / PROJECTS   **MIT***

O _____ : ☆

O _____ : ☆

O _____ : ☆

O _____ : ☆

O _____ : ☆

O _____ : ☆

O _____ : ☆

O _____ : ☆

O _____ : ☆

O _____ : ☆

***An MIT is a "Most Important Thing" Wirte only 10 things—Why try to do more? You'll be discouraged**

ME-TIME

PRE-SCHEDULED MEETINGS

REFLECTIONS, MEDITATIONS, THOUGHTS

PROCESS = PRODUCT

FAMILY / SOCIAL ORGANIZER DATE

MEAL PLANNER

TODAY'S TO-DO LIST   MIT*

○_____: ☆

○_____: ☆

○_____: ☆

○_____: ☆

○_____: ☆

○_____: ☆

○_____: ☆

○_____: ☆

○_____: ☆

○_____: ☆

*An MIT is a "Most Important Thing" Wirte only 10 things—Why try to do more? You'll be discouraged

TOMORROW'S AGENDA   **SOMETIME THIS WEEK**

NOTES, THOUGHTS, REFLECTIONS

PROCESS = PRODUCT

FAMILY / SOCIAL ORGANIZER DATE

MEAL PLANNER

TODAY'S TO-DO LIST   **MIT***

○ _____ : _____   ☆

○ _____ : _____   ☆

○ _____ : _____   ☆

○ _____ : _____   ☆

○ _____ : _____   ☆

○ _____ : _____   ☆

○ _____ : _____   ☆

○ _____ : _____   ☆

○ _____ : _____   ☆

○ _____ : _____   ☆

***An MIT is a "Most Important Thing" Wirte only 10 things—Why try to do more? You'll be discouraged**

TOMORROW'S AGENDA   **SOMETIME THIS WEEK**

NOTES, THOUGHTS, REFLECTIONS

PROCESS = PRODUCT

FAMILY / SOCIAL ORGANIZER DATE

MEAL PLANNER

TODAY'S TO-DO LIST   **MIT***

○_____: ☆

○_____: ☆

○_____: ☆

○_____: ☆

○_____: ☆

○_____: ☆

○_____: ☆

○_____: ☆

○_____: ☆

○_____: ☆

***An MIT is a "Most Important Thing" Wirte only 10 things—Why try to do more? You'll be discouraged**

TOMORROW'S AGENDA   **SOMETIME THIS WEEK**

NOTES, THOUGHTS, REFLECTIONS

PROCESS = PRODUCT

BUSINESS / FINANCIAL ORGANIZER DATE

TODAY'S FINANCIAL STEPS TO SUCCESS

ABOUT MY FATHER'S BUSINESS (BUSINESS PRIORITIES) MIT*

○_____: ☆

○_____: ☆

○_____: ☆

○_____: ☆

○_____: ☆

○_____: ☆

○_____: ☆

○_____: ☆

○_____: ☆

○_____: ☆

*An MIT is a "Most Important Thing" Wirte only 10 things—Why try to do more? You'll be discouraged

NEEDS VS WANTS

PRE-SCHEDULED MEETINGS

HOW I SAVED AND GAVE

PROCESS = PRODUCT

BUSINESS / FINANCIAL ORGANIZER

DATE

TODAY'S FINANCIAL STEPS TO SUCCESS

ABOUT MY FATHER'S BUSINESS (BUSINESS PRIORITIES)

MIT*

○ _____: ☆

○ _____: ☆

○ _____: ☆

○ _____: ☆

○ _____: ☆

○ _____: ☆

○ _____: ☆

○ _____: ☆

○ _____: ☆

○ _____: ☆

*An MIT is a "Most Important Thing" Wirte only 10 things—Why try to do more? You'll be discouraged

NEEDS VS WANTS

PRE-SCHEDULED MEETINGS

HOW I SAVED AND GAVE

PROCESS = PRODUCT

BUSINESS / FINANCIAL ORGANIZER   DATE

TODAY'S FINANCIAL STEPS TO SUCCESS

ABOUT MY FATHER'S BUSINESS (BUSINESS PRIORITIES)   MIT*

○ _____ : ☆

○ _____ : ☆

○ _____ : ☆

○ _____ : ☆

○ _____ : ☆

○ _____ : ☆

○ _____ : ☆

○ _____ : ☆

○ _____ : ☆

○ _____ : ☆

*An MIT is a "Most Important Thing" Wirte only 10 things—Why try to do more? You'll be discouraged

NEEDS VS WANTS

PRE-SCHEDULED MEETINGS

HOW I SAVED AND GAVE

PROCESS = PRODUCT

VISION BOARD = PRODUCT

DEATH AND LIFE ARE IN THE POWER OF THE TONGUE

Introduction to Salvation

"For God so loved the world, that he gave His only begotten son, that whosoever believeth in Him should not perish, but have everlasting life. God did not send His Son into the world to condemn the world; but to save the world." (John 3:16-17).

I have six very important questions to ask:

1. Have you made Jesus Christ your personal Lord and Savior? (Romans 10:9-10)
2. Did you know that Jesus came to destroy the works of the devil in your life? (1 John3:8)
3. Did you know that Jesus is the Light of the world? (John 9:5)
4. If you died today, where would you spend eternity – in heaven or hell? (Romans 10:9)
5. Did you know that God so loved the world that he gave His only begotten Son so that we would have life and not death? (John 3:16)
6. Did you know that Jesus loves you? (John 15:9)

Jesus Christ is Lord

If you have already received Jesus Christ as your personal Lord and Savior, praise the Lord! You can be assured that if you died today you will go directly to heaven to be with the Father. If you have not confessed Jesus Christ as you personal Lord and Savior, I invite you to say this very simple prayer.

Prayer of Salvation

Repeat this prayer aloud:

Dear Lord,

I come to you now just as I am. You know my life and you know how I have lived. Forgive me Lord; I repent of my sins. I believe that Jesus Christ died for my sins and on the third day, He was raised from the dead. Lord Jesus, I ask you to come into my heart. Live your life in me and through me. From this moment forward, I belong to you Lord. I renounce the devil and I confess Jesus Christ as my personal Lord and Savior. In the name of Jesus, Amen!

Congratulations!

If you said this prayer, the Bible says in II Corinthians 5:17, "Therefore if any man be in Christ, he is a new creature, old things are passed away behold, all things are made new." Translation, "you have a brand new start on life!"

Begin to spend time in your Bible, start a daily life of prayer, and ask God to lead you to a church where you can grow and have a better knowledge and understanding of the Word of God.

I would like to leave you with one of my favorite scriptures in the Bible. It says in Proverbs 3:5-6, "Lean on, trust in, and be confident in the Lord with all your heart and mind and do not rely on your own insight or understanding. In all your ways know, recognize, and acknowledge the Lord and He will direct and make straight and plain your path."

I encourage you to seek God before making any decisions in your life. Believe God when He says that His thoughts and plans for you are good and not evil. Trust God when He says in Ecclesiastes 7:8, "The end of anything is better than its beginning."

Take a moment to think about all the work you have done in this book thus far. Now, close your eyes for the next 5-10 minutes and envision yourself full of confidence and posessing a good attitude. See yourself doing the impossible. See yourself accomplishing your goals and being successful. See yourself living out your purpose and being fulfilled. See the Finished Work – You!

Email your testimony to tdwayne@teamunstoppable.solutions. Include your name, city, and phone number. Also, let us know if we can share your testimony with others on the website and in future publications/materials.

www.ingramcontent.com/pod-product-compliance
Lightning Source LLC
LaVergne TN
LVHW081349060426
835508LV00017B/1488